COMPREHENSIVE

BEST KARATE
Comprehensive

M. Nakayama

KODANSHA USA

Front cover photo by Keizō Kaneko.

Published by Kodansha USA Publishing, LLC
451 Park Avenue South, New York, NY 10016

Distributed in the United Kingdom and continental Europe
by Kodansha Europe Ltd.

ISBN: 978-1-56836-463-6
LCC 77-74829

First edition published in Japan in 1977 by Kodansha International
First US edition 2012 by Kodansha USA,
an imprint of Kodansha USA Publishing, LLC

26 25 24 23   8 7 6

www.kodansha.us

CONTENTS

Dedicated
to my teacher
GICHIN FUNAKOSHI

INTRODUCTION

The past decade has seen a great increase in the popularity of karate-dō throughout the world. Among those who have been attracted to it are college students and teachers, artists, businessmen and civil servants. It has come to be practiced by policemen and members of Japan's Self-defense Forces. In a number of universities, it has become a compulsory subject, and that number is increasing yearly.

Along with the increase in popularity, there have been certain unfortunate and regrettable interpretations and performances. For one thing, karate has been confused with the so-called Chinese-style boxing, and its relationship with the original Okinawan *Te* has not been sufficiently understood. There are also people who have regarded it as a mere show, in which two men attack each other savagely, or the contestants battle each other as though it were a form of boxing in which the feet are used, or a man shows off by breaking bricks or other hard objects with his head, hand or foot.

If karate is practiced solely as a fighting technique, this is cause for regret. The fundamental techniques have been developed and perfected through long years of study and practice, but to make any effective use of these techniques, the spiritual aspect of this art of self-defense must be recognized and must play the predominant role. It is gratifying to me to see that there are those who understand this, who know that karate-dō is a purely Oriental martial art, and who train with the proper attitude.

To be capable of inflicting devastating damage on an opponent with one blow of the fist or a single kick has indeed been the objective of this ancient Okinawan martial art. But even the practitioners of old placed stronger emphasis on the spiritual side of the art than on the techniques. Training means training of body and spirit, and, above all else, one should treat his opponent courteously and with the proper etiquette. It is not enough to fight with all one's power; the real objective in karate-dō is to do so for the sake of justice.

Gichin Funakoshi, a great master of karate-dō, pointed out repeatedly that the first purpose in pursuing this art is the nurturing of a sublime spirit, a spirit of humility. Simultaneously, power sufficient to destroy a ferocious wild animal with a single blow should be developed. Becoming a true follower of karate-dō is possible only when one attains perfection in these two aspects, the one spiritual, the other physical.

Karate as an art of self-defense and karate as a means of improving and maintaining health has long existed. During the past twenty years, a new activity has been explored and is coming to the fore. This is *sports karate.*

In sports karate, contests are held for the purpose of determining the ability of the participants. This needs emphasizing, for here again there is cause for regret. There is a tendency to place too much emphasis on winning contests, and those who do so neglect the practice of fundamental techniques, opting instead to attempt jiyū kumite at the earliest opportunity.

Emphasis on winning contests cannot help but alter the fundamental techniques a person uses and the practice he engages in. Not only that, it will result in a person's being incapable of executing a strong and effective technique, which, after all, is the unique characteristic of karate-dō. The man who begins jiyū kumite prematurely—without having practiced fundamentals sufficiently—will soon be overtaken by the man who has trained in the basic techniques long and diligently. It is, quite simply, a matter of haste makes waste. There is no alternative to learning and practicing basic techniques and movements step by step, stage by stage.

If karate competitions are to be held, they must be conducted under suitable conditions and in the proper spirit. The desire to win a contest is counterproductive, since it leads to a lack of seriousness in learning the fundamentals. Moreover, aiming for a savage display of strength and power in a contest is totally undesirable. When this happens, courtesy toward the opponent is forgotten, and this is of prime importance in any expression of karate. I believe this matter deserves a great deal of reflection and self-examination by both instructors and students.

To explain the many and complex movements of the body, it has been my desire to present a fully illustrated book with an up-to-date text, based on the experience in this art that I have acquired over a period of forty-six years. This hope is being realized by the publication of the *Best Karate* series, in which earlier writings of mine have been totally revised with the help and encouragement of my readers. This new series explains in detail what karate-dō is in language made as simple as possible, and I sincerely hope that it will be of help to followers of karate-dō. I hope also that karateka in many countries will be able to understand each other better through this series of books.

WHAT KARATE-DŌ IS

Deciding who is the winner and who is the loser is not the ultimate objective. Karate-dō is a martial art for the development of character through training, so that the karateka can surmount any obstacle, tangible or intangible.

Karate-dō is an empty-handed art of self-defense in which the arms and legs are systematically trained and an enemy attacking by surprise can be controlled by a demonstration of strength like that of using actual weapons.

Karate-dō is exercise through which the karateka masters all body movements, such as bending, jumping and balancing, by learning to move limbs and body backward and forward, left and right, up and down, freely and uniformly.

The techniques of karate-dō are well controlled according to the karateka's will power and are directed at the target accurately and spontaneously.

The essence of karate techniques is *kime*. The meaning of *kime* is an explosive attack to the target using the appropriate technique and maximum power in the shortest time possible. (Long ago, there was the expression *ikken hissatsu,* meaning "to kill with one blow," but to assume from this that killing is the objective is dangerous and incorrect. It should be remembered that the karateka of old were able to practice *kime* daily and in dead seriousness by using the makiwara.)

Kime may be accomplished by striking, punching or kicking, but also by blocking. A technique lacking *kime* can never be regarded as true karate, no matter how great the resemblance to karate. A contest is no exception; however, it is against the rules to make contact because of the danger involved.

Sun-dome means to arrest a technique just before contact with the target (one *sun,* about three centimeters). But not carrying a technique through to *kime* is not true karate, so the question is how to reconcile the contradiction between *kime* and *sun-dome*. The answer is this: establish the target slightly in front of the opponent's vital point. It can then be hit in a controlled way with maximum power, without making contact.

Training transforms various parts of the body into weapons to be used freely and effectively. The quality necessary to accomplish this is self-control. To become a victor, one must first overcome his own self.

Above: Officials of the International Amateur Karate Federation at the world tournament, Los Angeles, U.S.A., 1975.

Left: The honorary president and the chairman of the Karate-dō Institute of Indonesia, 1974. (Gen. Surono and Mr. Sabeth, respectively)

Left: Karate-dō competitors, Denmark, 1975.

1
BASICS

NATURAL WEAPONS

The weapons of karate-dō are various parts of the human body, Every part that can be effective in defense or offense is used, It is in this respect that karate-dō is different from the other martial arts.

Systematic training is the only way to develop weapons that will be ready for use at any time, in any place, in any situation. It is most important that training of every part of the body be continuous and methodical. Intensive training alone is not adequate to convert the parts of the body into powerful weapons.

Making a Fist

The two ways of using the hand are (1) open and (2) closed. There are six types of fists (*ken*) and eleven types of open-hand (*kaishō*).

To make a fist, start by folding the fingers so that the tips reach only to the base of the fingers. Then continue to fold the fingers inward until the tips are pressed tightly into the palm. Press the thumb firmly over the second joints of the index and middle fingers. The little finger is apt to become weak and relaxed, so it is necessary to be careful about keeping it pressed tightly against the palm.

A second way, not used much nowadays, is to first fold the middle, ring and little fingers, then press the index finger slantwise over the middle finger. This has fallen into disuse because of the difficulty of getting used to it and the tendency of the little finger to become relaxed.

Types of Fists

Seiken   *Fore-fist*

The knuckles of the index and middle fingers are used to strike the target. The wrist must be kept tense and unbent, the back of the hand and the wrist forming a straight line. The primary use is in the thrust punch (*tsuki*). All the power of the arm must be concentrated and flow in a straight line to the knuckles.

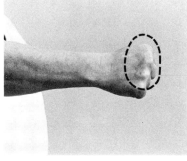

Uraken   *Back-fist*

The back of the hand and knuckles of the index and middle fingers are used primarily for striking (*uchi*). Using the spring-like power of the elbow, strikes are made in a sideward or vertically rising movement. Targets are primarily the opponent's face or the side of his body.

16

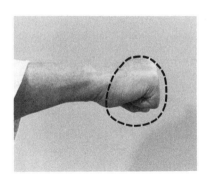

Kentsui   *Hammer Fist*

Attacks to the body are delivered with the bottom (little finger side) of the fist.

Other names for this fist are *shutsui* (hammer hand) and *tettsui* (iron hammer).

Ippon-ken   *One-knuckle Fist*

With the middle, ring and little fingers the same as in the fore-fist, the middle knuckle of the index finger is extended and the thumb pressed against it. The bridge of the nose, the point just below the nose and the space between the ribs are the usual targets for this fist.

17

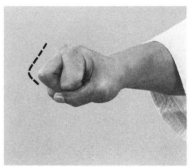

Nakadaka-ken   *Middle Finger Knuckle Fist*

This resembles the fore-fist, but the middle joint of the middle finger is extended and the index and ring fingers are pressed tightly against the middle finger. The thumb presses against the index and middle fingers. Primary targets are the bridge of the nose, the point below the nose and the space between the ribs.

This fist is also called *nakadaka-ippon-ken* (middle finger one-knuckle fist).

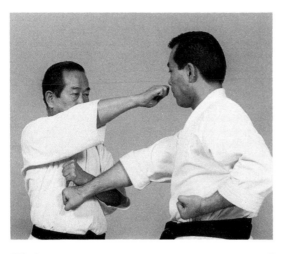
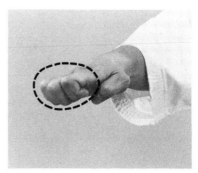

Hiraken   *Fore-knuckle Fist*

The fingers are bent until the tips just touch the palm, and the thumb is held tightly against the index finger. The knuckles are used to attack between the ribs or the point just below the nose.

18

Types of Open Hands

The extended fingers of the open-hand (*kaishō*) must be pressed tightly together, and the back of the hand and the wrist must form a straight line. The thumb is bent and held tightly against the palm, It is important that the base of the thumb should not be deeply bent.

Shutō — *Sword Hand*

With the fingers straight and tight together, the outer edge of the palm is used like a sword, either to block or attack. Targets include the temple, the carotid artery and the ribs.

Haitō — *Ridge Hand*

The form of the hand is the same as the sword hand, but the opposite edge, centered on the base joint of the index finger, is used. It is used for the same purposes as the sword hand.

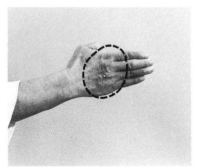

Haishu   *Back-hand*

The whole surface of the back of the open-hand may be used to strike, but for the most part it is used in blocking.

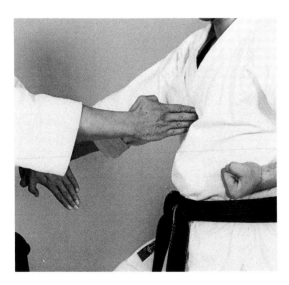

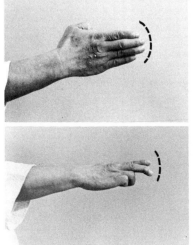

Nukite   *Spear Hand*

The fingers are tense, with the tips slightly bent. In either a sideward or a rising motion, an attack can be made to the ribs, side of the body, solar plexus or the point below the nose.

Only two fingers can also form a spear hand, the middle and index fingers, or the index finger and thumb. In this case it is called two-finger spear hand (*nihon nukite*).

Teishō   *Heel of the Palm*

This is formed from the open-hand by bending the wrist back fully. It is useful in sweeping an opponent's attacking arm to one side or downward. In attacks, it is very effective for strikes to the jaw.

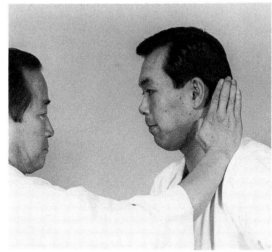

Seiryūtō   *Ox Jaw Hand*

By bending the hand sideways, the edge of the palm and the wrist come to form a curve. Then the palm below the little finger can be effective in blocking the opponent's forward thrust or in attacking his face or collarbone.

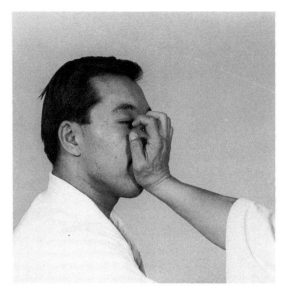

Kumade   *Bear Hand*

The fingers are folded so that the tips just touch the palm. The thumb is also folded. The entire surface of the palm is directed in a powerful attack against the face.

Washide   *Eagle Hand*

The tips of the fingers and thumb are brought together so as to resemble a bird's peak. They are then used for attacks to the throat or other vital points.

Keitō   *Chicken Head Wrist*

The hand is bent outward, with the thumb bent at the joint and the fingers flexed. The striking surface is the thumb from its base to the knuckle. It can be used effectively against the opponent's attacking arm or his armpit.

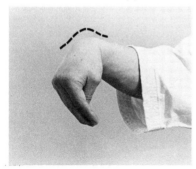

Kakutō   *Bent-wrist*

By bending the hand inward to the fullest extent, the wrist can become a powerful weapon. It can be used against the opponent's punching arm or to strike his armpit.

Ude   Arm

Blocking is the most important function of the forearm. All four surfaces are used: inner side (*naiwan*), outer side (*gaiwan*), upper side (*haiwan*) and lower side (*shuwan*).

The forearm is also referred to as *wantō* (*sword arm*) and *shubō* (stick arm).

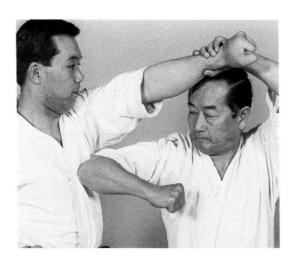 

Hiji or Empi   Elbow

Powerful blows with the elbow can be delivered to the face, chest, side of the body and so on. The basic types of attack are the forward elbow strike (*mae empi-uchi*), upward elbow strike (*tate empi-uchi*), back elbow strike (*ushiro empi-uchi*), roundhouse elbow strike (*mawashi empi-uchi*) and downward elbow strike (*otoshi empi-uchi*).

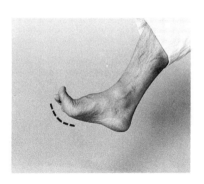

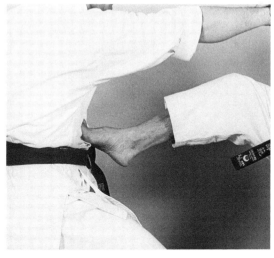

Koshi   *Ball of the Foot*

The toes are turned upward to the maximum extent possible, and tension is kept in the toe joints and the ankle. Kicks are directed to the jaw, chest, stomach, groin and so on.

Another name for this weapon is *jōsokutei* (raised sole).

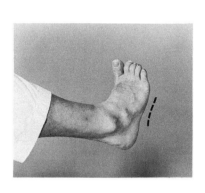

Sokutō   *Sword Foot*

With the toes curled upward and the ankle fully bent, the outer edge of the foot is used for the side kick.

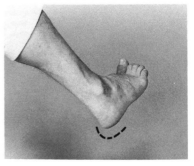

Kakato   *Heel*

The heel is used for back kicks.
It is also called *enshō* (round heel).

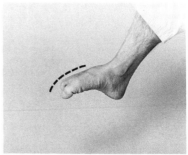

Haisoku   *Instep*

With the ankle stretched, the foot and toes are bent fully downward. The instep is particularly useful for kicks to the groin.

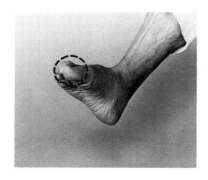

Tsumasaki   *Toe Tips*

The toes are kept tightly together, and kicks are made with the tips. Primarily this is used against the midsection.

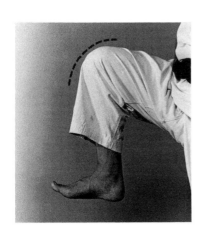

Hizagashira   *Knee*

Like the elbow, the knee is most useful when the opponent is at close range. Targets include the groin, the side of the body and the thigh.

As a weapon, this is also known as *shittsui* (hammer knee).

STANCES

Fundamental to the improvement of one's karate technique is the acquisition of correct and balanced form.

Stance, as a term, must be thought of with regard to the lower part of the body. For techniques to be fast and accurate, powerfully and smoothly executed, the stance must be strong and stable.

At all times, the upper part of the body must be kept perpendicular to the ground and the hips level. The joints should not be overly tense, no more strength than is necessary should be used in excuting a technique, and it is desirable that the stance be relaxed.

Shizen-tai   *Natural Position*

In the natural position, the body is relaxed but in a state of alertness, ready to cope with any situation. The knees must be relaxed and flexible at all times, so that one can shift instantly to any defense or attack position.

The position of the feet varies in the several forms of the natural position, but the principle of alert relaxation remains the same.

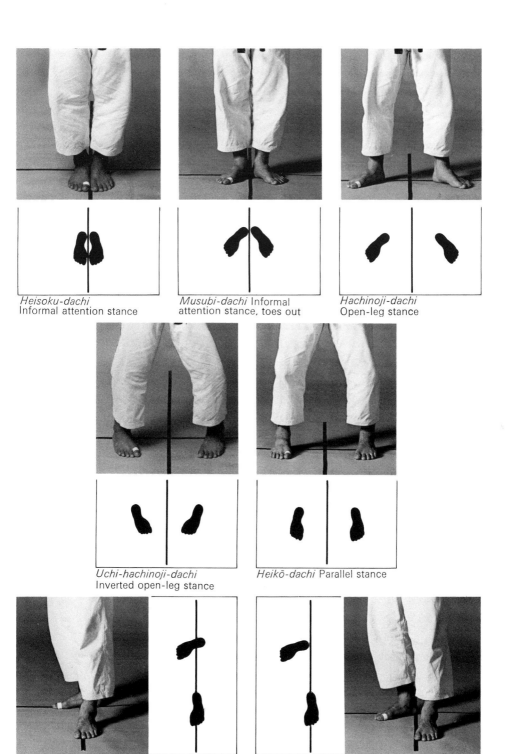

Heisoku-dachi
Informal attention stance

Musubi-dachi Informal
attention stance, toes out

Hachinoji-dachi
Open-leg stance

Uchi-hachinoji-dachi
Inverted open-leg stance

Heikō-dachi Parallel stance

Teiji-dachi T stance

Renoji-dachi L Stance

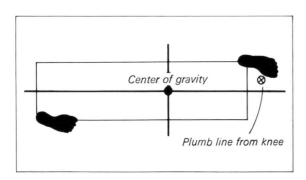

Center of gravity

Plumb line from knee

Zenkutsu-dachi   Front Stance

The back leg is straight, the front leg is bent so that the knee is directly over the foot, and the hips are lowered. The back must be kept directly over the hips and perpendicular to the ground. Face directly forward. The distribution of weight between the front and rear feet is in the ratio of 6 to 4.

In the *hanmi* (half-front-facing) variation of this stance, the torso is at a 45° angle to the front, with the head facing forward.

This is a strong position for attacks to frontal targets.

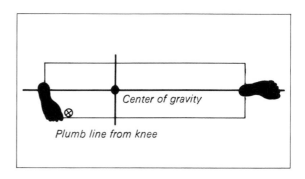

Center of gravity

Plumb line from knee

Kōkutsu-dachi   *Back Stance*

The feet are spread apart with the knee of the back foot bent and the front leg stretched lightly forward. The hips are lowered, and the back is kept straight in a half-front-facing position. The distribution of weight between the front and back feet is in the ratio of 3 to 7.

This stance is effective for blocking frontal attacks.

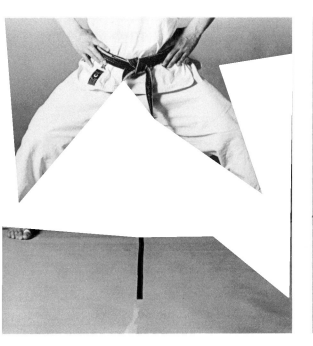
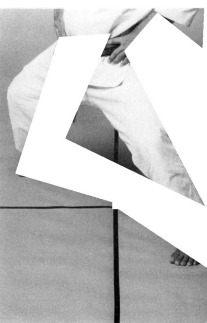
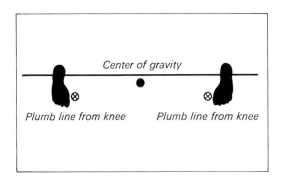

Center of gravity

Plumb line from knee   Plumb line from knee

Kiba-dachi   *Straddle-leg Stance*

When the feet are spread to the sides, the heels must be kept on a straight line and the weight evenly distributed between the two feet. The hips are lowered directly downward, the back is straight and perpendicular to the ground, and the body faces directly forward.

The straddle-leg stance is basic in the acquirement of stable posture and in the training of the legs and hips. It is effective for attacking targets to the left or right sides.

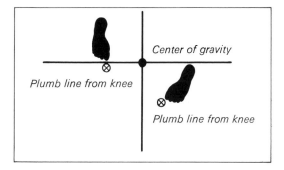

Center of gravity

Plumb line from knee

Plumb line from knee

Sanchin-dachi   *Hourglass Stance*

The feet are spread to the sides, with the front foot slightly forward. Both knees are bent and turned inward. The lower abdomen is tense, and the upper body straight and perpendicular to the ground. If the feet are too close together or the knees bent too much inward, stability will be impaired and flexibility lost.

This is a strong stance for executing techniques either to the front or rear or to the left or right, particularly defensive techniques.

 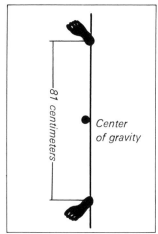

Shiko-dachi   *Square Stance*

This is like the straddle-leg stance except that the feet are outward at 45° angles and the hips are lower.

Like the straddle-leg stance, it is good for training the legs and hips and is a strong position for carrying out offensive techniques to the sides.

 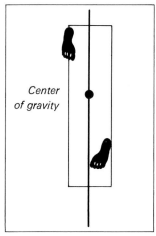

Hangetsu-dachi   *Half-moon Stance*

This stance resembles the front stance in the placing of the feet and the hourglass stance in the turning inward of the knees and in other points. It may be regarded as being halfway between the two.

It is effective in both defense and attack, but tends to be used more for defense.

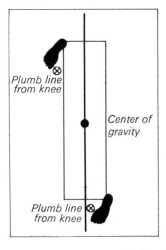

Fudō-dachi   *Rooted Stance*

The knees are fully bent as in the straddle-leg stance, but the position of the feet is different.

This is a strong position from which one can block an attack and immediately go on the offensive.

It is also known as *sōchin-dachi.*

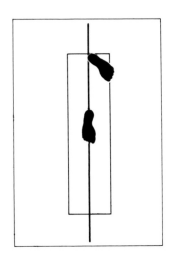

Neko-ashi-dachi   *Cat Leg Stance*

With the front knee turned slightly inward and the heel raised, most of the body weight is supported by the rear leg, the knee of which is also bent. The rear foot is pointed diagonally forward.

From this stance, one can quickly move out of range of an attack and immediately counterattack.

Training in Stances

Shizen-tai hachinoji-dachi
Open-leg stance

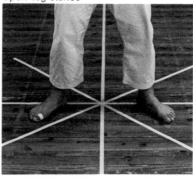

Migi kiba-dachi Right straddle-leg stance

Hidari kiba-dachi Left straddle-leg stance

Migi zenkutsu-dachi Right front stance

Hidari zenkutsu-dachi Left front stance

Migi fudō-dachi Right rooted stance

Hidari fudō-dachi Left rooted stance

Rooted stance to the rear

Rooted stance to the rear

Right back stance diagonally to the rear

Left back stance diagonally to the rear

Right back stance to the rear

Left back stance to the rear

Shizen-tai Natural position

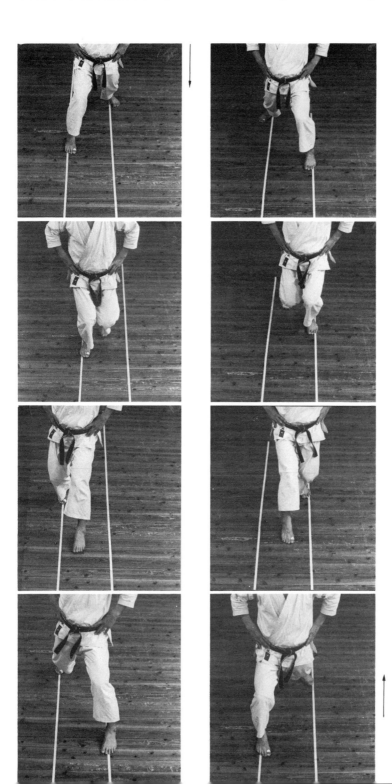

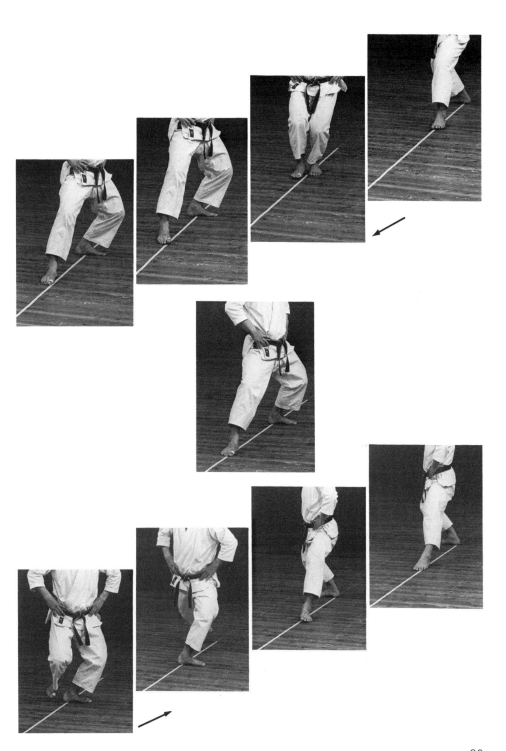

PREPARATORY EXERCISES

By oneself

Salvador, Brazil, 1975.

Dōjō of the East Coast Karate Association, United States.

2
PRINCIPLES

PRINCIPLES OF KARATE TECHNIQUES

The basic techniques of blocking, punching, striking and kicking are both the beginning of karate-dō and the ultimate goal. Although only a matter of months may be sufficient to learn them, complete mastery may not come even after a lifetime of training. The student must practice regularly, with maximum concentration and effort in the execution of each and every movement.

This will not be sufficient, however, unless the techniques are scientifically sound and the training systematic and properly scheduled. To be effective, training must be conducted on the basis of correct physical and physiological principles.

It may come as a surprise to many to know that the techniques created and refined through long and continuous practice by the early karateka have been found to accord with modern scientific principles. And the more they are studied, the more this proves to be true. This is not to say that there are no unsolved problems, but these must await further study. Further refinement of karate-dō is quite probable, as techniques are analyzed in an unceasing effort to improve them through a scientific approach.

In order to benefit from his training, the student should have a good understanding of the following primary points.

Correct form is always closely related to the principles of physics and physiology.

In baseball, the homerun hitter always has excellent form. And the beauty of the master fencer's form nears perfection. These are clearly the result of long practice and soundly based training.

Prerequisites of correct form are good balance, a high degree of stability and the order of movements of each part of the body, since movements are made in quick succession in a short period of time.

This is especially true in karate because punching and kicking are vital to the art. The need for good balance can be seen particularly in kicking, where the body is usually supported by one leg. To withstand the great impact when a blow is landed, stability of all joints in the arms and hands is necessary.

With changing situations and different techniques, the center of gravity changes, shifting to the left, right, front, back. This cannot be done unless the nerves and muscles are well trained. Again, standing on one foot for too long will open one to attack, so balance must be constantly shifted from one foot to the other. The karateka must both avoid giving an opening and be prepared for the next attack.

Power accumulates with speed. Muscular strength alone will not enable one to excel in the martial arts, or in any sport for that matter. The power of the *kime* (finish) of a basic karate technique derives from the concentration of maximum force at the moment of impact, and this in turn depends greatly on the speed of the blow or kick. The punch of a highly trained karateka can travel at a speed of thirteen meters per second and generate power equivalent to seven hundred kilograms.

Though speed is important, it cannot be effective without control. Speed and power are increased by utilizing the pairing of forces and reaction. For this purpose, an understanding of the dynamics of movement and their application is necessary.

Concentration and Relaxation of Power

Maximum power is the concentration of the strength of all parts of the body on the target, not just the strength of the arms and legs.

Equally important is the elimination of unnecessary power when executing a technique, which will result in giving greater power where it is needed. Basically, power should start at zero, climax to one hundred on impact, and immediately return to zero. Relaxing unnecessary power does not mean relaxing alertness. One should always be alert and prepared for the next movement.

Strengthening of Muscular Power

Understanding of theory and principles without strong, well-trained, elastic muscles to execute the techniques is useless. Strengthening muscles requires constant training.

It is also desirable to know which muscles are used in which techniques. To the extent that muscles are used specifically, greater effectivess can be expected. Conversely, the less muscles are used unnecessarily, the less the loss of energy. Muscles operating fully and harmoniously will produce strong and effective techniques.

Rhythm and Timing

In any sport, the performance of a top athlete is very rhythmical. This applies also in karate.

The timing of various techniques cannot be expressed musically, but it is nonetheless important. The three principal factors are the correct use of power, swiftness or slowness in executing techniques and the stretching and contraction of muscles.

The performance of a master karateka is not only powerful but very rhythmical and beautiful. Acquiring a sense of rhythm and timing is an excellent way to make progress in the art.

Hips

The hips are located approximately at the center of the human body, and their movement plays a crucial role in the execution of various types of karate techniques. The explosive power of the finishing blow is created by the lower abdomen, particularly the rotation of the hips, which adds to the power of the upper body.

Besides being a source of power, the hips provide the basis for a stable spirit, correct form and maintenance of good balance. In karate, the advice is often given to "punch with your hips," "kick with your hips," and "block with your hips."

Breathing

Breathing is coordinated with the execution of a technique, specifically, inhaling when blocking, exhaling when a finishing technique is executed, and inhaling and exhaling when successive techniques are performed.

Breathing should not be uniform; it should change with changing situations.

When inhaling, fill the lungs full, but when exhaling, do not expel all the air. Leave about 20 percent in the lungs. Exhaling completely will leave the body limp. One will not be able to block even a weak blow, nor will he be able to prepare for the next movement.

3
TRAINING

BASIC TECHNIQUES

HAND AND ARM TECHNIQUES

Karate differs from boxing and other fighting arts in defensive techniques. There are many techniques for blocking kicks, and these make use of the legs and feet as well as the hands and arms. Karate is unique in this respect.

All blocks must be executed at the very beginning of the opponent's attack. Therefore, it is absolutely necessary to anticipate the attack. The various purposes of blocking should be kept in mind.

1. *To discourage further attack.* The use of great force can deter the opponent from further attacks, and in this way the block itself becomes an attack.

2. *To parry.* An attacking arm or leg can be blocked lightly, with only enough force to deflect it.

3. *To block and attack.* It is possible to block and counterattack at the same instant.

4. *To unbalance the opponent.*

5. *To withdraw.* After blocking, one can take a position of safety until there is an opportunity for counterattack.

Mastery of the following points is essential to effective blocking techniques.

1. *Direction of power.* It is impossible to block without first having accurately assessed the path of the attack. Deflect the strike or kick by blocking: from underneath upward, if the attack is to the head or upper torso. From inside outward or from outside inward, if the attack is to the chest. Downward and sweeping outward, if the attack is to the abdomen.

2. *Forearm rotation and timing.* Merely hitting the attacking arm is comparatively weak. Rotating the forearm of the blocking arm makes the block stronger, but good timing is critical.

3. *Hip rotation.* Rotating the hips is as much a part of blocking as it is of punching. Block and finish with the hips, withdrawing the other arm at the same time that the block is made.

4. *Position of the elbow.* An effective block depends on concentrating all body power in the forearm at the moment of contact. When the elbow is touching the body, the power is greatest, but this tends to reduce the scope of the block. Depending on the situation, the elbow should be neither too close nor too far from the side of the body—in principle, at a distance about equal to the width of the fist.

5. *Effects of overblocking.* Overblocking results in loss of balance, loss of tension in the side muscles, reduction of body control and difficulty in excuting follow-up techniques. It is necessary to learn the appropriate position for each blocking technique.

6. *Block-attack.* Besides the option of inhibiting further attacks by blocking with great force, there are several blocking techniques that in themselves become finishing blows.

Egypt, 1975

Gedan Barai   Downward Block

This is both a basic block and one of the preparatory positions in basic training.

Against a strike or kick to the abdomen or groin, use the wrist in blocking downward and to the side.

1. Use the elbow as a pivot, straighten the arm as you block in a big downward motion, and bring the fist about fifteen centimeters above the knee of the forward leg at the finish.

2. Both forearms rotate, and the two arms should almost touch as they pass each other.

3. Against a strong upward kick, block strongly.

Jōdan Age-uke   *Upper Block against Head Attack*

This is a basic block used to counter attacks aimed above the solar plexus. Block upward, strongly, with the outer side of the forearm.

1. The arms cross at chin height, the blocking arm outside, the withdrawing arm inside. Move the arms crisply and powerfully, keeping the elbow of the blocking arm in a 90° angle.

2. Complete the block with the forearm about 10 centimeters in front of the forehead, fist higher than the elbow, palm outward. Keep the elbow close to the body.

3. The fist is tightened at the moment of blocking, at which time the abdominal muscles should be strongly tightened. In a wavelike flow of power, this tension should be transmitted to the muscles around the armpit, then to the blocking arm.

Chūdan Ude Uke   *Forearm Block against Body Attack*
Soto-uke   *Outside inward*

This is used against a punch aimed at the chest or face. Deflect the opponent's arm to the side, blocking with the outer edge of the wrist.

1. At the finish, be sure that the elbow of the blocking arm is bent at about a 90° angle and the forearm is almost perpendicular to the ground. The forearm and the side of the body should be roughly aligned, i.e., avoid overblocking.

2. Fist in front of the chin, the elbow should be about ten centimeters in front of the body and the muscles around the armpit tense.

3. Bring the other arm back to the side and form a tight fist. Rotate the hips in the direction of the block, utilizing the power to strike the attacking arm with great force.

Chūdan Ude Uke	*Forearm Block against Body Attack*
Uchi-uke	*Inside outward*

A punch aimed at the chest or face can be blocked with the inner edge of the wrist.

1. The path of the blocking arm is outside the withdrawing arm.

2. The other points given with regard to the outside-inward forearm block are also applicable here.

Shutō Uke   Sword Hand Block

This is a basic defensive technique against an attack directed to the abdomen, chest or face. The edge of the hand is wielded in a slantwise motion, as if the intention were to cut off the opponent's arm.

1. The other hand, instead of being brought to the side, is positioned in front of the solar plexus with the palm facing upward. Thus it can be used immediately after the block for a spear hand counterattack to the opponent's midsection.

2. From a point beside the ear, the blocking hand is brought forward and diagonally downward. The blocking hand passes over the forearm of the other hand; the withdrawing hand passes below the elbow of the blocking arm.

3. At the completion of the technique, the elbow of the blocking arm should form a right angle, and the muscles around the armpit should be tensed. Take care that the arm does not go to far out, i.e., not beyond the side of the body.

4. Not stepping backward or stepping straight backward will make the block ineffective. Therefore, step back diagonally.

Tate Shutō-uke   *Vertical Sword-hand Block*

While sweeping the forearm from the inside outward, bend the wrist, pointing the fingers straight up with the palm forward. This is useful against punches to the chest or solar plexus. Unlike the other sword-hand block, the elbow is kept straight.

This technique can be carried out effectively by taking a side step or by sliding one foot forward and approaching the opponent.

Kake Shutō-uke   *Hooking Sword-hand Block*

With the wrist bent lightly, the forearm is swung widely from inside outward to hook-block the opponent's wrist. It is often possible to grasp his wrist after blocking. As with the vertical sword-hand block, this technique can be effective against an attack from the side as well as one from the front.

Haishu-uke Back-hand block

Haiwan nagashi-uke
Sweeping back-arm block

Te nagashi-uke
Sweeping hand block

Te osae-uke
Pressing hand block

Tekubi kake-uke
Hooking wrist block

Maeude hineri-uke
Twisting forearm block

Maeude deai-osae-uke
Pressing forearm block

Haishu uke   Back-hand Block

Using the spring-power of the elbow, block with the back-hand. Keep the hand and wrist straight, and concentrate power on the back surface of the hand. This is to counter a punch to the chest or solar plexus by hitting the opponent's upper arm, elbow or forearm.

Other blocking techniques are : dropping block (*otoshi-uke*), sweeping back-arm block (*haiwan nagashi-uke*), sweeping hand block (*te nagashi-uke*), pressing hand block (*te osae-uke*), hooking wrist block (*tekubi kake-uke*), twisting forearm block (*maeude hineri-uke*) and pressing forearm block (*maeude deai-osae-uke*).

Kakutō uke Bent-wrist block

Keitō uke Chicken-head wrist block

Seiryūtō uke Ox-jaw hand block

Teishō uke Heel of the palm block

Kakutō Uke   Bent-wrist Block

A forearm can be blocked strongly with this, either by striking upward or by deflecting it to the side.

Keitō Uke   Chicken-head Wrist Block

This is used to block the opponent's forearm from underneath upward.

Seiryūtō Uke   Ox-jaw Hand Block

With this, a forearm or leg is blocked with a downward swing.

Teishō Uke   Heel of the Palm Block

Forearm or leg can be deflected upward, downward or from one side to the other.

63

Two-hand Blocks

Morote uke Augmented forearm block

Sokumen awase-uke Side combined block

Ryōshō tsukami-uke Two-hand grasping block

Jūji uke X block

Kakiwake-uke Reverse wedge block

Gedan kake-uke Downward hooking block

Shō sukui-uke Scooping palm block

Teishō awase-uke
Combined heel of the palm block

Sokutei mawashi-uke Circular sole block

Sokutō osae-uke Pressing sword-foot block

Sokutei osae-uke Pressing sole block

Sokubō kake-uke Hooking foot block

Ashikubi kake-uke Hooking ankle block

Attacking

Attacking with the hands or elbows is of two types: punching (*tsuki*) and striking (*uchi*)

Tsuki	*Punching*

Most commonly, this term refers to the straight punch (*choku-zuki*), though there are other types.

When the opponent is directly in front of you, the arm is straightened and the target is punched with the knuckles of the fore-fist. The forearm is rotated inward during the delivery of the punch.

Depending on the objective—face, solar plexus or abdomen—these techniques are known as: upper straight punch (*jōdan choku-zuki*), middle straight punch (*chūdan choku-zuki*) or lower straight punch (*gedan choku-zuki*).

In any case, for the punch to be effective, the following basic factors must be learned and put into practice.

1. *Correct route.* The shortest distance is the straight-line route, and this is the correct way to punch. At the same time that the elbow brushes the side of the body lightly, the forearm should be rotated inward.

2. *Speed.* Without great speed, the punch cannot be expected to have much effect. To maximize speed and power, withdraw the other arm as fast as possible, thus making use of the pairing of forces.

3. *Concentration of Power.* A good punch depends on starting from a flexible posture and keeping unnecessary strength out of the hand and arm. Punch smoothly but speedily, concentrating all the power of the body at the moment of impact. The concentration of power must be mastered. Practice by raising the arms in front of the body, holding the fists level with the solar plexus, and repeatedly tensing and relaxing all the body muscles.

Correct route of straight punch

Methods of Punching

Gyaku-zuki   Reverse Punch

The advanced leg and fist are on opposite sides. When the left leg is in front, punch with the right fist. This is primarily for counterattacking after a block but is powerful only when the rotating hips are brought into full play. The height of the hips and keeping them level is most important. Straightening the rear leg and shifting the pelvis and center of gravity forward slightly make the punch strong.

Effective practice lies in having the rotation of the hips and upper body lead the arm movement.

Oi-zuki   Lunge Punch

From either the natural position or a front stance, move into a front stance by sliding one foot forward, punching at the same time with the fore-fist on the side of the advancing foot. Utilize to the fullest the reaction from extending the supporting leg and from rotating the hips forward. The foot should be slid smoothly and rapidly without raising the heel.

The lunge punch can be more devastating than the reverse punch.

Nagashi-zuki   Flowing Punch

This can be executed from the half-front-facing position by stepping diagonally either forward or backward. Power comes from the movement of the body, and it is especially effective for a combined block-attack.

Kizami-zuki   Jab

Without moving the front leg, jab by forcefully straightening the arm, using the hips and rear leg for power. It can be decisive, but more often it is used as a diversionary tactic to be followed by a lunge punch, reverse punch or other finishing blow.

Ren-zuki   Alternate Punching

This is punching alternately with the left and right fists, using either reverse punch or lunge punch (two or three times).

Punch repeatedly with the same fist by bending and extending the elbow rapidly.

Morote-zuki *Two-hand Punch*

This is punching simultaneously with both fists, either parallel with each other or one above the other.

Gyaku-zuki Reverse punch

Oi-zuki Lunge punch

Types of Punches

Tate-zuki Vertical punch

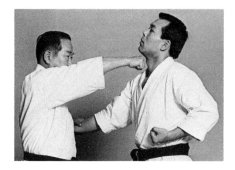

Age-zuki Rising punch

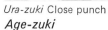

Ura-zuki Close punch

Age-zuki   Rising Punch

This is a punch from the hips upward, the fist following a half-circle route. Use the fore-fist, especially the knuckles of the index and middle fingers against the face or chin.

Ura-zuki   Close Punch

Using the fore-fist, punch straight ahead, bringing the palm inward or upward. Targets are the face, midsection or side of the body. If the side muscles are not tensed, the punch will not be effective.

Kagi-zuki   Hook Punch

The fore-fist is employed with the elbow fully bent. Targets to the side (solar plexus or side of the body) are attacked at a right angle. When stepping forward and to the side for this punch, the side muscles tend to relax. Pay special attention to keeping them tensed.

Mawashi-zuki   Roundhouse Punch

Attack the face, side of the head or side of the body; the fore-fist rises from the hip in a half-circular movement. Since there is a strong tendency for the elbow to leave the side of the body, take care to synchronize the arm with the hip rotation and brush the elbow against the body.

71

Awase-zuki	*U Punch*

Both fore-fists are used, straight punch (palm downward) to the face, close punch (palm upward) to the abdomen. Punch simultaneously, straight upward, bringing the power of the body into full play.

Yama-zuki	*Wide U Punch*

In a half-front-facing position, lower the forward shoulder. Keep the head midway between the arms. With the elbow slightly bent, the upper arm follows a slightly curved path to the face. The lower arm travels a nearly straight path to the abdomen, with the elbow in a position so that it could be braced with the hip. Punch simultaneously with the fore-fists, upper palm downward, lower palm upward.

This is a variation of the U punch.

Heikō-zuki   *Parallel Punch*

This is directed against the intercostal area below the nipples. Using power from the body, punch straight forward with both fore-fists hitting the targets at the same time.

Hasami-zuki   *Scissors Punch*

From the hips, the fore-fists take a half-circle path, outward, then inward. Effectiveness will be lost if the elbows come to far away from the body. Punch both sides of the opponent's body simultaneously.

Striking

In punching, the elbow is straightened and the forearm extended. Striking with the hand involves bending and straightening the elbow. With the elbow as the pivot, the forearm moves as though one were drawing semicircles, but swiftly and forcefully, making full use of the snap of the elbow.

Both the fist and the open-hand are used, as in the back-fist strike (*uraken-uchi*), hammer fist strike (*kentsui uchi*), sword hand strike (*shutō uchi*) and so on.

The elbow can also be used to strike. The arm is fully bent, and the elbow is aimed at the target. This is especially valuable for fighting at close quarters, when freedom of movement of the arms, legs or body has been lost, or when you are grasped from behind.

The important point in striking is the use of the snap of the arm. There should be no strength in the shoulder, and the fist or fingers of the open hand should be tightly closed. Strike in a wide curve with maximum speed.

Uraken-uchi	Back-fist Strike
Kentsui-uchi	Hammer Fist Strike

Using the snap of the elbow, strike in an arclike path, either horizontally or vertically. Primarily, this is for a counterattack to the face, solar plexus or side of the body.

1. Use the elbow like a spring. The fist must be tightly clenched, and to the maximum extent possible, reduce strength from the elbow.

2. In a horizontal strike (*yoko mawashi-uchi*), the forearm is parallel to the floor. In a vertical strike (*tate mawashi-uchi*), it becomes perpendicular to the floor.

3. It is absolutely necessary that the elbow point in the direction of the target. Besides snap, effectiveness depends on the path of the fist being correct and the length of the arc reaching its maximum.

Uraken-uchi tatemawashi
Vertical back-fist strike

Uraken-uchi yokomawashi
Side roundhouse back-fist
strike

Kentsui-uchi hammer-fist strike

Elbow strikes can be made to the front, back or sides—rising, falling or turning to the side—when movement of the torso is restricted, you are grasped from behind, or the opponent has grabbed your arm.

Of course, they differ from hand strikes; they should be regarded as *ate-waza*, i.e., smashing techniques. They are also known as *empi uchi* (elbow strikes).

The following points are the important ones:

1. Although effective as a counterattack at close range, it is a mistake to aim at a target very far away.

2. Keep the upper body erect and use the rotation of the hip. If the torso is off the perpendicular, the strike may not be ineffective, but it will give the opponent the advantage.

3. Not keeping the fist and forearm close to the body will weaken the strike. Brush the arm against the body as it moves.

4. Effectiveness and power come from rotating the forearm and bending the elbow deeply.

Tate hiji-ate Upward elbow strike

Mae hiji-ate Forward elbow strike

Yoko hiji-ate Side elbow strike

Yoko mawashi hiji-ate
Side roundhouse elbow strike

77

Mae Hiji-ate   Forward Elbow Strike

For a strike with the right elbow, the right fist comes from the right hip to the left nipple, always touching the body. The forearm too should be kept as close to the body as possible.

This is for attacking the chest or abdomen of a frontal target, especially if you have been grabbed from the front.

It is also called *mae empi-uchi.*

Yoko Hiji-ate   Side Elbow Strike

Keeping the forearm close to the chest, so that it brushes the nipples, move it in a perfectly straight line in the direction of attack. Use the power of the body.

This is a counterattack especially useful when you are grabbed from the side or when the opponent attacks from the front, then moves to the side. Targets are the chest or the side of the body.

It is also called *yoko empi-uchi.*

Ushiro Hiji-ate — Back Elbow Strike

Attack directly to the rear with the elbow, strongly and decisively. It is important that the fist come to the side of the body.

Targets are the opponent's chest or midsection, particularly when he attempts to grab you from the rear.

This is also called *ushiro empi-uchi.*

Yoko Mawashi Hiji-ate — Side Roundhouse Elbow Strike

This is a counterattack made after disposing of a frontal attack. For a right elbow strike, the right fist is placed in front of the right nipple; strike strongly, coordinating the elbow with the rotation of the hips and the forward movement of the body.

The target is the side of the face or chest.

This is also called *yoko mawashi empi-uchi*

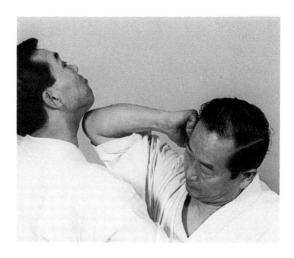

Tate Hiji-ate   *Upward Elbow Strike*

To be effective, the forearm must be kept close to the body as it is raised into a vertical position, and since the upper body tends to twist, care must be taken to rotate the hips in a plane parallel to the floor and to keep the torso perpendicular.

Blocking a frontal attack while stamping forward, counter-attack to the chin or abdomen.

This is also called *tate empi-uchi.*

Otoshi Hiji-ate	*Downward Elbow Strike*

Immediately after the opponent is thrown or pulled downward, strike from above not with the elbow but with the force of the whole body. The forearm must be kept vertical as the hips are lowered, and attention given to the stability of the lower body.

Counterattack directly downward, hitting the face, back of the head or trunk.

This is also called *otoshi empi-uchi.*

Haitō-uchi Ridge-hand strike

Shutō Uchi　　　　　　　　　　　　　*Sword Hand Strike*

As in the back-fist strike, the snap of the elbow and the rotation of the forearm and hips are main points.

Rotate the forearm fully, so that the palm comes to face in the opposite direction at the time of striking.

Attacks can be made either from the inside outward or the outside inward. When from inside outward, rotate the hips in the opposite direction from the strike; when outside inward, same direction. Always rotate the hips swiftly.

Principle targets are the temple, carotid artery and side of the body.

The ridge hand can also be used for this technique.

Uchi mawashi-uchi
Roundhouse strike, inside outward

Soto mawashi-uchi
Roundhouse strike, outside inward

FOOT AND LEG TECHNIQUES

Kicking is as important in karate as hand techniques; in fact, a kick has more power than does the fist.

Good balance is all-important, not only because all of the body weight is supported by one leg but because of the countershock on impact. Having the sole of the supporting foot wholly and firmly planted and tensing the ankle sufficiently are absolutely essential to maintaining balance.

When kicking, one should have the feeling of putting the whole body into it. Use the hips fully, but withdraw the kicking leg quickly and take up the position for the next technique. Otherwise, the opponent may succeed in scooping or catching the leg.

The length of the arc the foot travels, the speed and the snapping power of the knee determine the force of the kick. Of particular importance is the muscular power employed in straightening the knee.

To master kicking, one must understand the primary factors and continue to practice systematically.

1. *Bending the knee.* Raise the kicking leg straight up, bringing the knee, fully bent, high and shifting the weight of the leg toward the hips. Mastering this movement, which should be done quickly but lightly, is useful in producing a strong, sharp kick.

2. *Snap, bending and straightening of the knee.* There are two ways of kicking: (1) using the springlike power of the knee by snapping it fully and (2) strongly straightening the knee.

In the snap kick, after the knee is raised, the kneecap becomes the center of a semicircular movement. Speed is of the essence; without it, the kick cannot not be sharp, and balance will be destroyed.

In the thrust kick (*kekomi*), the knee, in the raised position, is forcefully straightened, kicking to the front, diagonally to the front and downward, to the side or diagonally to the side and downward.

3. *Spring of the hips and ankle.* In either type, the power of the leg by itself is not sufficient. To this must be added the spring of the hips and knee. For this purpose, the ankles must, of course, be made strong through extended training.

Mae keage Front snap kick

Mae kekomi Front thrust kick

Mae-geri   *Front Kick*

This may be either a snap kick or a thrust kick. The opponent's face, chest, abdomen or groin is attacked with the ball of the foot, the toes or the instep.

Keage   *Snap Kick*

Fully bending and raising the knee of either the front leg or the back leg to chest level, kick with a strong snapping motion. The foot follows a rising arclike path with the kneecap as the pivot. After kicking, bring the leg back to the inner side of the supporting leg, taking particular care throughout to keep the hips and upper body straight. The ball of the foot is commonly used, but the toes and instep may also be used.

Always face the target squarely for attacks to the face, chin, chest, groin or thigh.

Kekomi   *Thrust Kick*

Using the ball or heel of the foot, straighten the leg forcefully from the raised-knee position. Effectiveness comes from keeping the lumbar vertebrae facing forward and using the power of the hips. This is good for a downward slanting kick. Targets are the solar plexus, groin, thigh or lower leg.

Yoko keage Side snap kick   *Yoko kekomi* Side thrust kick

Yoko-geri   Side Kick

While keeping the upper body facing forward, the sword foot can be used against a target to the side. It is either a snap kick or a thrust kick, depending on the situation.

Keage   Snap Kick

This is a counterattack against an attack from the side, but the edge of the foot may be used for blocking too.

Kick with the heel, using the snap of the knee that has been raised to chest level. Bend the ankle fully upward, To get the necessary, strong support of the other leg, bend the ankle so the kneecap is directly over the toes and keep the leg firm.

Kekomi   Thrust Kick

Kick to the jaw, armpit, side of the body or groin.

It is necessary that the path of the foot in both kicking and withdrawing be the same. Using the sword foot, deliver the power of the hips as well as of the snap of the knee, which is, of course, raised as high as possible. The longer the distance the foot travels, the stronger the kick.

This is directed against the face, midsection, chest, side of the body or thigh of an opponent to the side.

For a target at close hand, there are variations of the thrust kick: *fumikiri* (cutting kick) and *fumikomi* (stamping kick).

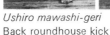
Ushiro mawashi-geri
Back roundhouse kick

Mawashi-geri	*Roundhouse Kick*

To be effective, the hips must be rotated strongly and swiftly. Against a target in front or slightly to the side, kick with either the front or back leg. Swing the leg in an arc from outside inward, using the snap of the knee. The path of the leg should be nearly parallel to the floor.

The ball of the foot or instep is used against the face, neck, chest or side of the body.

It is also possible to attack the opponent's solar plexus or the side of his body by kicking from inside outward in what is known as the *gyaku mawashi-geri* (reverse roundhouse kick).

Ushiro-kekomi   *Back Thrust Kick*

While facing forward, snap kick or thrust kick to the rear, using either leg. Positioning the target, maintaining stability and not being thrown off balance when the kick lands are difficult, so the supporting leg must be well planted and firm.

This is effective when you are being grasped or attacked directly from the rear. Aim for the face, solar plexus, abdomen, groin, thigh or leg.

Another way of kicking is in an arc from outside inward.

Nidan-geri Two-level kick

Tobi-geri	*Jump Kick*

There are several variations of this powerful technique of kicking from the top of a high jump.

Kicking with the rear leg.

Springing upward with the rear leg and kicking with the front leg.

Combination front kick: Making a short sharp kick to the middle level with one leg, then immediately following with a big kick to the upper level. This is called *nidan-geri* (two-level kick).

Thrust kicking to the side and downward with the sword foot in the *tobi yoko-geri* (jumping side kick).

None of these are easy. First it is necessary to master the front kick, side kick and combination kicks. When the time comes for learning the jump kick, start practice from a low-level jump and gradually increase the height.

Tobi-geri Jump kick

Tobi yoko-geri Jumping side kick

4
KATA

TYPES OF KATA

Blocking, punching, striking and kicking—the fundamental techniques of karate—are combined in a logical manner in the *kata*, the formal exercises. Since ancient times, the various kata have been the core of karate, having been developed and perfected by old masters through long training and experience.

The kata, about fifty of which have come down to the present day, can be roughly divided into two groups. On the one hand are those that are seemingly simple but also exhibit grandeur, composure and dignity. Through practice of this type of kata, the karateka can build up his physique, tempering his bones and forging strong muscles.

The other group is suggestive of the flight of a swallow and is appropriate for the acquisition of fast reflexes and quick movements.

Execution of each kata, that is, the leg movements, is along a predetermined performance line (*embusen*). Though one practices without a visible opponent, he should have in mind disposing of enemies coming from four directions—or eight directions—and the possibility of a changing performance line.

Since the kata contain all of the elements essential for exercising the whole body, they are ideal for that purpose. Practicing alone or in a group, anyone can follow this Way, in accordance with his own level of ability and regardless of age.

It is through these formal exercises that the karateka can learn the art of self-defense, enabling him to face a dangerous situation naturally and expediently. But the degree of skillfulness is the determining factor.

Characteristics of the kata are:

1. For each kata, the number of movements is fixed (twenty, forty, etc.). They must be performed in the correct order.

2. The first movement of the kata and the last movement must be executed at the same point on the performance line. The performance line has various shapes depending on the kata, such as, straight line, like the letter T, like the letter I, in the

shape of an asterisk (*), and so on.

3. There are kata that must be learned and kata that are optional. The former are the five Heian kata and the three Tekki kata. The latter are Bassai, Kankū, Empi, Hangetsu, Jitte, Gankaku and Jion. Other kata are Meikyō, Chinte, Nijūshiho, Gojūshiho, Hyakuhachiho, Sanchin, Tenshō, Unsu, Sōchin and Seienchin.

4. To perform a kata dynamically, three rules must be remembered and observed: (1) correct use of power, (2) speed of movement, fast or slow, and (3) expansion and contraction of the body. The beauty, power and rhythm of the kata depend on these three things.

5. At the beginning and at the end of the kata, one bows. This is part of the kata. When doing kata successively, bow at the very beginning and at the completion of the final kata.

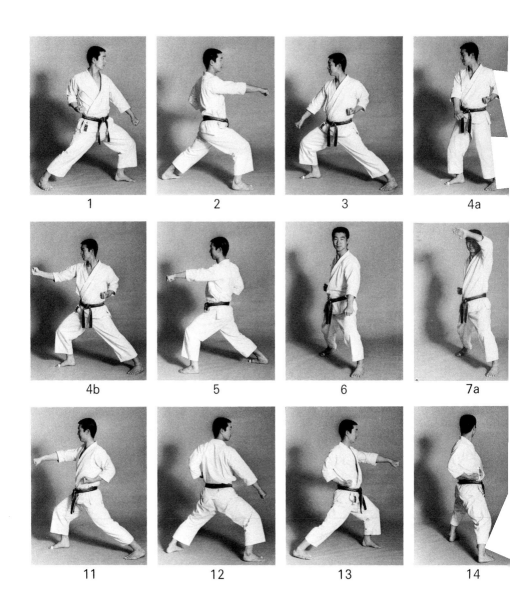

1   2   3   4a

4b   5   6   7a

11   12   13   14

Heian 1

The techniques in this kata are the upper block against head attack and the sword hand block against body attack (*chūdan shutō uke*). Because this is the first kata to be learned, it is important training in foot movements and following the performance line. In particular, aim for mastery of the front stance and back stance, while getting well acquainted with the essentials of the lunge punch.

The performance line is I shaped, the number of movements is twenty-one, and the time required is about forty seconds.

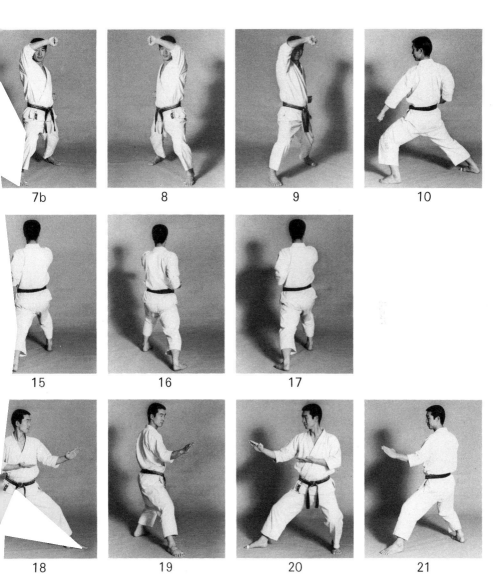

7b   8   9   10

15   16   17

18   19   20   21

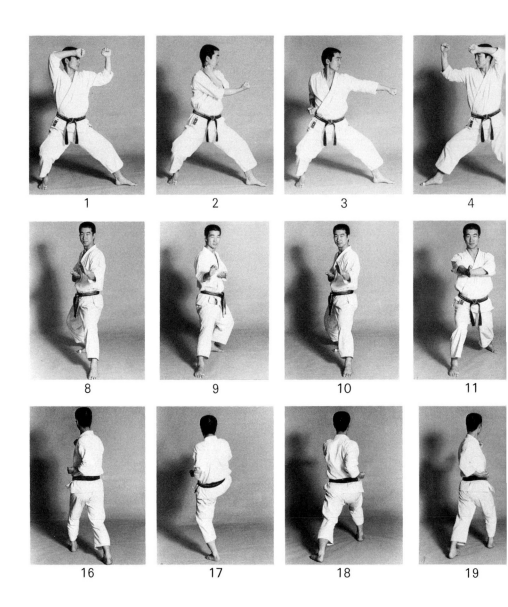

1   2   3   4

8   9   10   11

16   17   18   19

Heian 2

This is training in the side kick and front kick. Changing directions when executing a side kick is a particular point to be learned.

The performance line is **I** shaped, the number of movements is twenty-six, and the time required is about forty seconds.

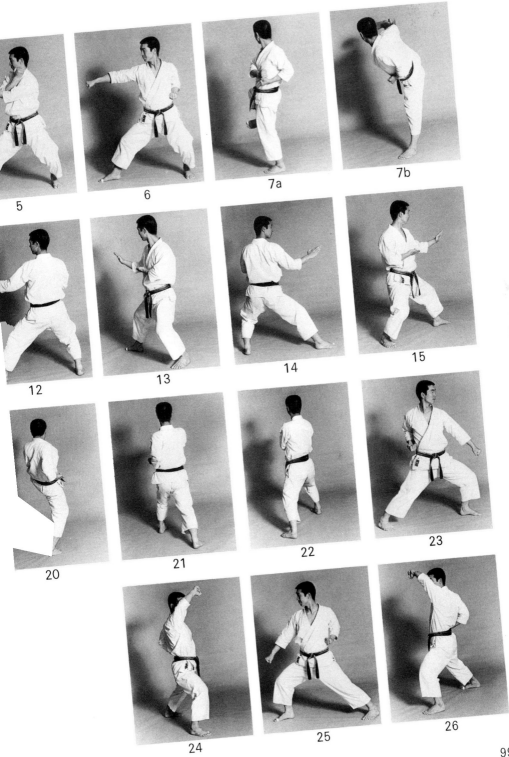

5

6

7a

7b

12

13

14

15

20

21

22

23

24

25

26

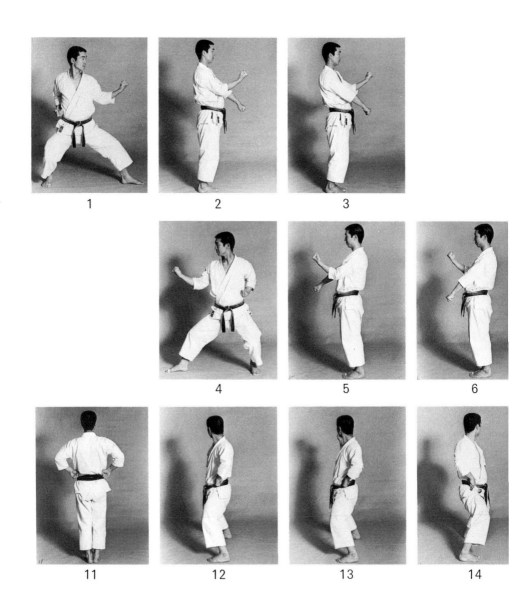

1   2   3

4   5   6

11   12   13   14

Heian 3

Mastery of the forearm block against body attack is the principal aim. With the elbow fully bent, learn to position it about a hand-width from the body with reliability.

Blocking with the elbow and counterattacking with a back-fist strike or elbow strike: from this kata, one can gain an understanding of the great value of this fundamental technique.

The performance line is T shaped, the number of movements is twenty, and the time required is about forty seconds.

7    8    9    10

15    16    17

18    19    20

1	2	3	4
9	10	11	12
17	18	19	20

Heian 4

Various blocking and finishing-off techniques can be learned from this kata, for example, jumping forward lightly for a vertical roundhouse back-fist strike after having made a front kick. To do this, it is necessary to have excellent balance in the crossed-feet stance (*kōsa-dachi*).

The performance line is in the shape of an I, but with the vertical line extending above the upper horizontal line. The number of movements is twenty-seven, and the time required is about fifty seconds.

5   6   7   8

13   14   15   16

21   22   23   24

25a   25b   26   27

1 2 3 4

6 7 8 9

14 15 16 17

Heian 5

The flowing water (*mizu-nagare*) position of the forearm, a special position, is used in this kata. This is for punching. Keep in mind that the forearm and chest should be parallel.

It is important to master balance, as when taking the crossed-leg stance when landing after a jump.

The performance line is T shaped, the number of movements is twenty-three, and the time required is about fifty seconds.

5

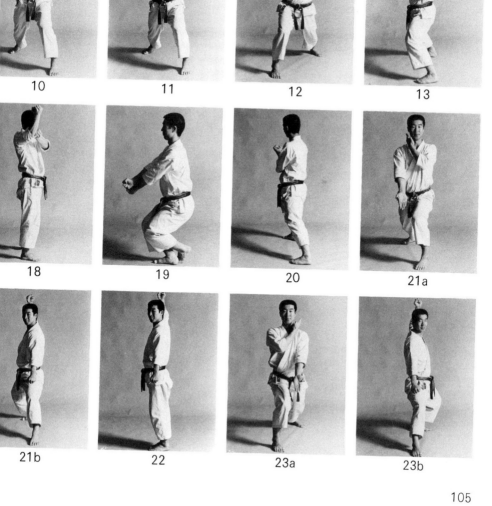

10

11

12

13

18

19

20

21a

21b

22

23a

23b

1   2   3   4

9   10   11   12

17   18   19   20

Tekki 1

The stance is the straddle-leg stance, and it is important that it be strong and stable. One's attitude should also show resolute intent.

For such special kicking techniques as the returning wave (*nami-gaeshi*) kick, the hips must be well set.

The performance line is a straight line, the number of movements is twenty-nine, and the time required is about fifty seconds.

25

5   6   7   8

13   14   15   16

21   22   23   24

26   27   28   29

107

Tekki 2   Tekki 3   Bassai

Tekki 2

A downward block to the side can be greatly strengthened by placing the hand of the other arm against the elbow of the blocking arm.

Make a clear distinction between the grasping block and the hooking block.

The performance line is a straight line, the number of movements is twenty-four, and the time required is about fifty seconds.

Tekki 3

From this kata, the key points of continuous middle-level blocking can be learned. No matter how fast the performance, the stance should be as strong and firm as in the other Tekki kata.

The performance line is a straight line, the number of movements is thirty-six, and the time required is about fifty seconds.

Bassai

Forcefulness, strong spirit and overflowing power are manifest in this kata. It is as though one were capturing an enemy castle. The karateka should know how to change disadvantage into advantage. Switching blocks and the right use of power are possible ways.

The performance line is T shaped, the number of movements is forty-two, and the time required is about one minute.

Kankū

Jitte

Hangetsu

Kankū

Imagine being completely surrounded by enemies. Fast techniques and slow techniques, techniques executed powerfully or softly, stretching and contraction of the body, jumping and crouching—these are the points in this kata.

The performance line is in the shape of an I, but with the vertical line extending above the upper horizontal line. The number of movements is sixty-five, and the time required is about ninety seconds.

Jitte

The movements in this kata are numerous, bold and grave and may be performed with a staff in the hands. It is appropriate for learning effective use of the hips and for blocking with the staff.

The performance line is cross shaped, the number of movements is twenty-four, and the time required is about one minute.

Hangetsu

Moving forward or backward, circular arm and leg movements are coordinated with breathing. Fast and slow techniques and sliding of the feet are particular points to be learned.

The performance line is cross shaped, the number of movements is forty-one, and the time required is about one minute.

Empi

Gankaku

Jion

Empi

Like the flight of a swallow, this kata has high and low positions, lightly and facilely performed. It is good for practicing the quick reversal of body positions.

The performance line is T shaped, the number of movements is thirty-seven, and the time required is about one minute.

Gankaku

Movements in this kata bring to mind a crane standing on one foot on a rock, ready to pounce on its prey. Balancing on one leg, the side kick and use of the back fist can be appropriately developed from practice of this kata.

The performance line is a straight line, the number of movements is forty-two, and the time required is about one minute.

Jion

Within the calm, smooth, harmonious movements of this kata lies a fierce fighting spirit. It is appropriate for learning such things as sliding the feet, shifting positions and turning.

The performance line is I shaped, the number of movements is forty-seven, and the time required is about one minute.

5
KUMITE

TYPES OF KUMITE

Kata and *kumite* are like the two wheels of a cart. The kata are practiced in order to learn techniques, offensive and defensive, and body movements; in this form of practice, the enemy exists only in the mind's eye. In *kumite*, another method of training, two men face each other and demonstrate techniques. Thus it can be considered an application of the fundamentals learned in the kata and may be said to be a kind of sparring.

In ancient days in Okinawa, karate was based almost exclusively on the kata. It was only rarely that the power of a punch or block was measured by what was called *kakedameshi*.

Following its introduction into Japan proper, karate gradually became popular among young men and was, inevitably, influenced by the Japanese martial arts. Basic kumite, which first came to be practiced in the late 1920s, was studied and refined, and jiyū kumite (free sparring) was developed. Today, kumite is widely practiced as a means of training.

Since kumite came into existence only after karate was introduced into Japan proper, it is, comparatively speaking, a new aspect of this art of self-defense. Thus, just as our predecessors of long ago took upon themselves the task of perfecting the kata, it is the duty of today's karateka to develop kumite to the same high level as the kata.

The three types of kumite are basic kumite, ippon kumite and jiyū kumite.

Basic kumite is for the cultivation of basic techniques, keeping in mind the individual student's level of skill.

Ippon kumite is for studying offensive and defensive techniques, training in body movements and learning *maai* (distancing).

In jiyū kumite, there is no prearrangement of techniques. The partners are allowed to make free use of their mental and physical powers, but the student must strictly control his punches, strikes and kicks. Actually making contact with the target is strictly prohibited, so the blow must be stopped just before it reaches the opponent's vital point. A well-trained karateka can do this easily, regardless of how powerfully executed the technique is.

Jiyū kumite has a strong appeal, perhaps because it is performed in dead earnest. The inexperienced person, however, attracted by and knowing only the surface aspects, will end up using his arms and legs mechanically, and the sparring will look like that of fighting cocks—or become a free-for-all. When this happens, the unique characteristic of karate-dō—destroying the enemy with a single, powerful blow—is lost. Moreover, it is a violation of the rules of karate-dō.

Without understanding *maai, kuzushi, kake, tsukuri* and strategy, the student cannot practice jiyū kumite. (In fact, much remains to be known about these, and development of karate along these lines is a task for the future.) Nor should he attempt jiyū kumite before having mastered basic kumite and ippon kumite.

Kumite is not something to be practiced instead of kata, which are, as they always have been, the most important, essential training.

The attacker, on the right, advances and attacks five times in successions. The blocker retreats and blocks five times, then counterattacks.

Gohon Kumite

In this type of sparring, the accuracy and power of strikes and blocks are to be learned, along with drill in foot movements.

There is also *sambon kumite*.

1

2

3

4

5

1

2

3

4

5

1

2

3

4

5

Lower level

1

2

3

4

5

1

2

3

4

5

Basic Ippon Kumite

The target is agreed upon beforehand, and the partners take turns attacking and defending. The objective is to learn how to make use of the offensive and defensive techniques and to understand distancing. This may be called the basic kata of sparring.

When the sudden attack comes, the block should be accurate and strong. As skill develops, the blocker should learn how to counterattack simultaneously. Blocking may be painful, but this should not be a excuse for engaging in haphazard sparring, which can lead to injury.

Block the attack to the body. Immediately make a roundhouse kick to the neck.

An attack to your chest. Step forward
and kick to the solar plexus.

Jiyū Ippon Kumite

Getting the feeling of distancing, blocking, attacking, body
movements, shifting of the center of gravity and delivering the
finishing blow are the objectives of this kumite. Here, in great
number, can be demonstrated the variations of the techniques
occurring in a single kata.

One partner, having announced the general area of his target,
attacks suddenly and with great strength. The other partner
blocks and counterattacks. Both men can freely demonstrate
all the techniques they know.

Both men must be well trained and highly skilled, for this
will seem like an actual fight. Neither should think of having a
second chance; the first attack, or block, is all.

This is the ultimate objective of karate training and the
preparatory stage for jiyū kumite.

Jiyū Kumite

Though nothing is prearranged and both men are expected to
exhibit their mental and physical powers at the highest level,
actual striking is prohibited, Blocks, blows and kicks must be
arrested before hitting the target, since the hands and feet of a
skilled karateka are extremely dangerous and can inflict fatal
injuries. Only the very well trained are capable of this.

124

After an attack to the head, counterattack with a right thrust kick.

A kick coming upward. Block with a downward X block.

Roundhouse kick, twisting left-arm block, right close punch.

A roundhouse kick coming at your head. Take out the opponent's supporting leg with a thrust kick.

Side kick against an attack to the face.

Right thrust kick against a body attack.

The opponent punches. Delivery a roundhouse kick to the face.

A front kick can be handled with a side thrust kick.

Block the attack to the face. Counter with a front kick.

Roundhouse kick against roundhouse kick. Who is faster?

Capetown, South Africa, 1975.

Montreal, Canada, 1974.

6
KARATE-DŌ

HISTORY

Tōte was first demonstrated publicly outside Okinawa in May, 1922, at the first National Athletic Exhibition, held in Tokyo under the sponsorship of the Ministry of Education. The man who was invited to give that memorable demonstration was Master Gichin Funakoshi, who at that time was president of the Okinawa Shobu Kai (society for the promotion of the martial arts).

Tōte (also called simply *Te*, meaning hand) was an art of self-defense that had been undergoing development in Okinawa for centuries. Because of the trade and other relationships between Okinawa and the Ming Dynasty in China, it is probable that it was influenced by Chinese fighting techniques, but there are no written records giving a clear idea of the development of *tōte*.

According to legendary accounts, Okinawa was unified under King Shōhashi of Chūzan in 1429, and later, during the reign of King Shōshin, an edict was issued prohibiting the practice of the martial arts. It is known that an order prohibiting weapons was promulgated by the Satsuma clan of Kagoshima, after they gained control of Okinawa in 1609. *Tōte* then became a last means of self-defense, but since the Satsuma clan also clamped down severely on this, it had to be practiced in great secrecy. For the Okinawans, there was no alternative, and they developed it into a deadly art as we know it today.

Not even a karateka's family would know that he was practicing this art, a situation which persisted until 1905, when the normal school in Shuri and the Prefectural First Middle School adopted karate as an official subject in physical education. However, its devastating power must have been known to some extent, for it was referred to by such terms as *Reimyō Tōte*, meaning miraculous karate, and *Shimpi Tōte*, meaning mysterious karate. That the secrecy itself greatly influenced the character of the art cannot be overlooked.

Tōte came to be known as *karate-jutsu*, and then, from around 1929, Gichin Funakoshi took the revolutionary step of strongly advocating that the name be changed to Karate-dō. Karate would thus be transformed, in both appearance and content, from techniques of Okinawan origin into a new Japanese martial art.

During the 1920s and early 1930s, this art of self-defense had been becoming increasingly popular with people from all strata of life. Students, of course, had been most enthusiastic, but there had also been lawyers, artists, businessmen, judoka, kendoka and many others. This was the dawning age of modern karate, and clubs were established successively at Keio University, Tokyo Imperial University, Shōka University, Takushoku University, Waseda University, Nihon College of Medicine and other schools in the Tokyo area. In 1930, with the arrival of Mabuni and Miyagi, teachers from Okinawa, clubs were formed at Ritsumeikan and Kansai universities in the Osaka area. The popularity among the intellectually inclined was very fortunate for karate, in that it helped in the transformation of the miraculous and mysterious karate into a modern, scientific martial art.

The name was not changed easily. Week after week, articles by Okinawan martial arts experts appeared in the *Okinawa Times* demanding to know *why*. In his eloquent style, Funakoshi replied, defending his position. This went on for some time.

With the publication of *Karate-dō Kyōhan* (by Master Funakoshi) in 1935, Karate-dō became firmly established. Two years after that, various karate societies in Okinawa joined the Japan Martial Arts Association, and a branch of the association was established in Okinawa.

I recall visiting Funakoshi during the time the controversy raged and reading the pros and cons. What struck me was the great enthusiasm and foresightedness of this master who was trying to disseminate a local art throughout the country as a whole.

Changing the name was not his sole concern. Many terms had only Chinese or Okinawan pronunciations. These he changed, too, making it possible for followers to understand them more easily. Training methods were another matter to which he gave his careful attention. Whereas previously there had been only kata, he now divided practice into three types: fundamentals, kata and kumite.

Young students gathered around Funakoshi and took to the practice of kumite with great enthusiasm. Kumite evolved from prearranged kumite to the practical jiyū ippon kumite and finally to jiyū kumite, where, so to speak, no holds are barred. The kata had become extremely refined in Okinawa. Now, research into kumite has improved considerably, and we may say that a new aspect of karate has been opened up. We may go further and say that karate today has almost reached the extreme point of perfection.

The first golden age of karate, as it has been called, occurred around 1940, when nearly every major university in Japan had its own karate club. In the early postwar years, it suffered a decline, but now, thanks to the enthusiasm of karate-dō supporters, it is being practiced more widely than ever. It has also spread to many countries throughout the world, creating a second golden age.

After the war. requests were frequently received from the Allied Forces stationed in Japan to see exhibitions of the martial arts. Judo, kendo and karate-dō experts formed groups and visited military bases two or three times a week to perform their respective arts. I still remember the great interest of the servicemen in karate, an art that they were seeing for the first time in their lives.

In 1952, the Strategic Air Command of the United States Air Force sent a group of young officers and noncommissioned officers to Japan to study judo, aikidō and karate-dō. The purpose of this was to train physical education instructors, and for the three months they were in Japan, they followed a stiff schedule, studying and practicing intensively. As the leader of the men teaching karate, I thought this was a great step forward for karate-dō. For more than a dozen years after that, two or three groups came every year.

This training program was evaluated highly, and groups began coming from other countries besides the United States. Various countries also requested that karate instructors be sent to train more instructors. This has, of course, been one influence in making karate popular around the world.

Karate is as it always has been an art of self-defense and a form of healthy exercise, but with the increase in popularity the interest in holding contests grew stronger, as it did in kendo and judo. Mostly due to the efforts of the younger enthusiasts, the First All-Japan Karate-dō Championship Tournament was held in October, 1957, This was sponsored by the Japan Karate Association, and the following month, the All-Japan Student Karate Federation sponsored a championship tournament before an audience numbering in the thousands. Besides being epoch-making events, these two tournaments created an even greater interest in the art throughout the country.

They are now held annually on an increasingly larger scale. And in a great number of countries, similar competitions are being held. At the peak of all these is the World Karate-dō Championship Tournament. The contests and the dissemination of karate abroad are the most significant developments in the postwar years.

Kata Contests

For kata, there are two ways of conducting the contest.

One is the red and white contest. In this, the contestants are divided into two groups, and one member from each group performs the same kata at the same time. After the completion of the kata, a flag, either red or white, is displayed to indicate the winner.

In the other way, points are given for each performance, ten points being the maximum. The contestant with the highest number of points becomes the winner.

Principal considerations in judging are power and spirit, but also moderation, and the three key points: correct use of power, appropriate speed of techniques and the stretching and contraction of the body. Points are forfeited for making mistakes in the order of movements and for not finishing the kata on the point on the performance line where it was begun.

No allowance is made for mistakes, however small. It is not always true that a person good at kata is the winner.

In a preliminary contest, a contestant is judged to be the winner if he scores an *ippon* within two minutes.

In a final contest, he must score three *ippon* in five minutes.

Timing of a strike, punch, kick or other finishing technique is an important factor in judging. When a contestant has not scored an *ippon* but has twice shown technique (*waza-ari*), these may be counted as one *ippon*. If neither contestant has clearly won, one may be declared winner by decision, or the contest may be declared a draw.

If a contestant actually makes contact with his opponent, he is guilty of a foul, since the responsibility is solely his, and he may lose on this basis. If the foul is only slight, however, he may receive a warning from the referee, with a deduction of points, and be allowed to continue.

Intensive training, mental and physical, is the prerequisite to being able to control one's movements, and this in turn is the mark of the skilled contestant. Just as in other sports and martial arts, the way to acquire this is through mastery of the basic techniques.

Practice with the makiwara is the soul of karate and should not be missed even for a single day. Its value lies not only in strengthening the parts of the body used in attacking and blocking but in learning to concentrate the power of the whole body in the fist at the time of impact. It is also an effective way to learn distancing.

Elasticity is the most important quality of the wood, *Hinoki* (Japanese cypress) is best, but *sugi* (Japanese cedar) will do. Because of its elasticity and absorbancy, rice straw is used to wrap the portion of the board that is hit. Rubber and sponge are possible substitutes.

Practice should be steady and diligent, rather than hurried, and strengthening of the body should be done by degrees. Hitting too quickly, or too suddenly, or too often may result in sprained wrists as well as broken skin.

Start by striking thirty times with the right fist and thirty times with the left fist. Increase the number gradually, until it reaches one hundred fifty, then eventually three hundred.

Thrust the forefist straight out, rotating the hips and using the snap of the elbow to the fullest. There is a shock at the moment of impact, and this has to be mastered. To be effective, the wrist must be tensed at impact. If the arm is used like a stick, the blow will not be effective.

1. In the front stance, picture the target as being one fist length in back of the makiwara. Distance is very important.

2. Do not lean forward. Straighten the elbow and thrust the fist far forward, bending the makiwara backward.

3. The elbow is bent slightly downward when the fist hits the makiwara squarely; at this point use the spring of the elbow and shoulder. The elbow becomes straight. When the makiwara returns to its original position, place the fist lightly on the surface and withdraw the elbow to the hip with the natural movement of the makiwara. Care should be taken that the elbow does not go too far out to the side.

4. The elbow, not the shoulder, should absorb the force of the makiwara springing back. The strike will be totally ineffective if the elbow or shoulders are tense or the body leans even slightly backward.

5. Practice using the rotation of the hips in the front stance. Then change from the immovable stance to the back stance to the front stance, using the movement and rotation of the hips. Gradually increase the speed of the strike.

Strengthening punching

The target should be one fist length in back of the makiwara. The course of the punch should be as long as possible. It is particular important to use centrifugal force.

1. For punching with the sword hand, back-fist or elbow, face the makiwara diagonally or sideways. Stances are the front stance, back stance and straddle-leg stance.

2. For use in inside and outside blocks, it is necessary to strengthen both the front and back of the wrists.

VITAL POINTS

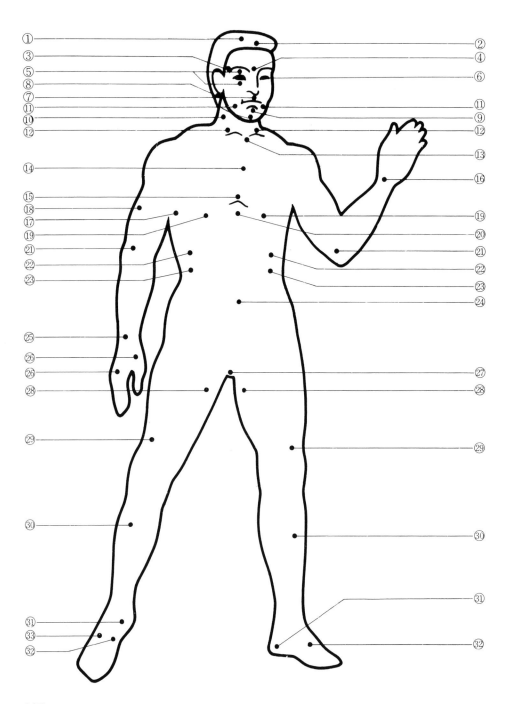

1. Coronal suture
2. Frontal fontanel
3. Temple
4. Glabella
5. Eye socket
6. Eyeball
7. Intermaxillary suture
8. Behind the ear
9. Center of lower jaw
10. Side of the neck
11. Mandible

MIDDLE REGION
12. Supraclavicular fossa
13. Suprasternal notch
14. Sternal angle
15. Xiphoid process
16. Inner side of the wrist
17. Fourth intercostal space
18. Back side of upper arm
19. Below the nipples
20. Solar plexus
21. Inner side of the elbow
22. Seventh intercostal space
23. Eleventh intercostal space
24. Point below the navel
25. Back of the wrist
26. Back of the hand

LOWER REGION
27. Testes
28. Inguinal region
29. Side of the lower thigh
30. Fibula
31. Medial malleolus
32. Instep
33. Outer side of the foot

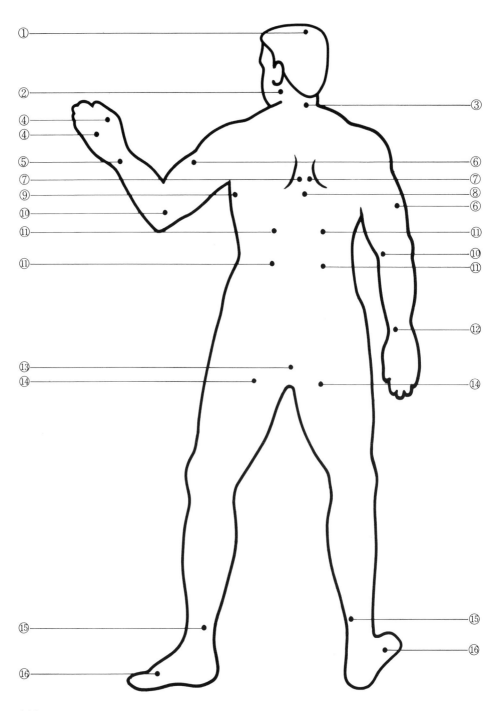

1. Coronal suture
2. Behind the ear
3. Third intervertebral space

MIDDLE REGION
4. Back of the hand
5. Back of the wrist
6. Back side of upper arm
7. Scapular ridge
8. Between fifth and sixth thoracic vertebrae
9. Fourth intercostal space
10. Inner side of the elbow
11. Ninth and eleventh thoracic vertebrae
12. Inner side of the wrist

LOWER REGION
13. Tip of the spine
14. Gluteal fold
15. Soleus muscle
16. Outer side of the foot

GLOSSARY

age-zuki: rising punch, 70
ashikubi kake-uke: hooking ankle block, 65
ate-waza: smashing technique, 77
awase-zuki: U punch, 72

choku-zuki: straight punch, 66
chūdan choku-zuki: middle straight punch, 66
chūdan shutō uke: sword hand block against body attack, 96
chūdan ude uke: forearm block against body attack; *soto-uke,* outside inward, 58; *uchi-uke,* inside outward, 59

dan-zuki: consecutive punching, 69

embusen: performance line, 94
empi: elbow, 24
empi uchi: elbow strike, 77
enshō: round heel, 26

fudō-dachi: rooted stance, 35
fumikiri: cutting kick, 87
fumikomi: stamping kick, 87

gaiwan: outer side of the forearm, 24
gedan barai: downward block, 56
gedan choku-zuki: lower straight punch, 66
gedan kake-uke: downward hooking block, 65
gyaku mawashi-geri: reverse round-house kick, 88
gyaku-zuki: reverse punch, 68

hachinoji-dachi: open-leg stance, 29
haishu: back-hand, 20
haishu uke: back-hand block, 62
haisoku: instep, 26

haitō: ridge hand, 19
haiwan: upper side of the forearm, 24
haiwan nagashi-uke: sweeping back-arm block, 62
hangetsu-dachi: half-moon stance, 34
hanmi: half-front-facing position, 30
hasami-zuki: scissors punch, 73
heikō-dachi: parallel stance, 29
heikō-zuki: parallel punch, 73
heisoku-dachi: informal attention stance, 29
hiji: elbow, 24
hiji-ate: elbow strike, 77
hiraken: fore-knuckle fist, 18
hizagashira: knee, 27

ippon-ken: one-knuckle fist, 17

jōdan age-uke: upper block against head attack, 57
jōdan choku-zuki: upper straight punch, 66
jōsokutei: raised sole, 25
jūji uke: X block, 64

kagi-zuki: hook punch, 71
kaishō: open-hand, 15, 19
kakato: heel, 26
kake shutō-uke: hooking sword-hand block, 61
kakiwake-uke: reverse wedge block, 64
kakutō: bent-wrist, 23
kakutō-uke: bent-wrist block, 63
keage: snap kick, 86, 87
keitō: chicken head wrist, 23
keitō uke: chicken-head wrist block, 63
kekomi: thrust kick, 86, 87
ken: fist, 15

143